Study Guide for Book Clubs: The Vanishing Half

KATHRYN COPE

CONTENTS

INTRODUCTION

There are few things more rewarding than getting together with a group of like-minded people and discussing a good book. Book club meetings, at their best, are vibrant, passionate affairs. Each member will bring along a different perspective, and ideally, there will be heated debate.

Nevertheless, a surprising number of book club members report that their meetings have been a disappointment. Even when their group enjoyed the book in question, they could think of astonishingly little to say about it and soon wandered off-topic altogether. Failing to find interesting discussion angles for a book is the single most common reason for book group meetings to fall flat. Most groups only meet once a month, and a lacklustre meeting is frustrating for everyone.

Study Guides for Book Clubs were born out of a passion for reading groups. Packed with information, they take the hard work out of preparing for a meeting and ensure that your book group discussions never run dry. How you choose to use the guides is entirely up to you. The 'Background', 'Style', and 'Setting' chapters provide useful context which may be worthwhile to share with your group early on. The all-important list of discussion questions, which will probably form the core of your meeting, can be found towards the end of this guide. To support your responses to the discussion questions, you will find it helpful to refer to the "Themes & Symbols," and "Character" sections.

A detailed plot synopsis is provided as an aide-memoire to recap on the finer points of the story. There is also a quick quiz—a fun way to test your knowledge and bring your discussion to a close. Finally, if this was a book that you enjoyed, the guide concludes with a list of further reads similar in style or subject matter.

This guide contains spoilers. Please do not be tempted to read it before you have finished the original novel as plot surprises will be well and truly ruined.

Kathryn Cope, 2020

BRIT BENNETT

Brit Bennett is an American writer. She grew up in Southern California and lives in Los Angeles.

Bennett took a Bachelor's in English at Stanford University. She then completed an MFA at the University of Michigan. While studying, she received the Hopwood Award for short fiction by graduates and the Hurston/Wright Award for College Writers.

In 2014, Bennett caught public attention with the essay, "I Don't Know What to Do With Good White People." First published on the blog *Jezebel*, the essay received over one million viewings in three days. The article discussed the issue of white people who claim to oppose racism but expect admiration for taking this stance. Bennett argued that it is easier to challenge overt racism than this form of white "self-aggrandizement."

Bennett's debut novel *The Mothers* was published in 2016 when the author was 26. The novel met with critical acclaim and was a *New York Times* bestseller. The author's second novel, *The Vanishing Half,* was released in 2020. It was an instant *New York Times* bestseller as well as a Good Morning America Book Club choice. In a reputed seven-figure deal, HBO swiftly acquired the rights to adapt the novel into a TV series.

BACKGROUND TO THE NOVEL

THE HISTORY OF PASSING

The Vanishing Half explores the history of 'passing' in the USA. Passing is when a person of colour deceives others into believing they are white. From the antebellum era onwards, many African Americans attempted to pass as white to improve their chances in life. In some cases, this was to avoid slavery or persecution. In others, it was to gain access to the social and economic privileges enjoyed by white Americans.

From the advent of slavery, the USA developed rigid systems of racial classification. Much of society's structure, such as slavery and segregation, was based upon maintaining a strict divide between black and white. For this reason, the notion of 'invisible whiteness' was an ongoing concern. If black Americans were sufficiently light-skinned, what was to stop them from seamlessly assimilating into white society?

During the early twentieth century, anxiety about black Americans crossing the 'colour line' increased. The Great Migration partly prompted this unease. When thousands of African Americans moved from the rural South to more northerly cities, the social landscape of the country dramatically changed. Concerns about the dangers of racial fluidity led to the introduction of the one-drop rule. This legal guideline stated that if a person had just one African American ancestor (i.e. "one drop" of black blood), they were to be categorised as black.

The introduction of the one-drop rule emphasised just how fiercely American society defended white privilege. The legal classification gave credence to the idea of 'passing' as a fraudulent crime. Nevertheless, many Americans who met the one-drop rule decided that it was worth taking the risk of passing. For obvious reasons, the number of black Americans who successfully passed themselves off as white is unknown. However, it is estimated that in the first two decades of the twentieth century, more than 300,000 people of colour crossed the "colour line."

In 1925, the politics of passing were highlighted in a scandalous trial known as the Rhinelander Case. Leonard Rhinelander—a wealthy white socialite—was persuaded by his family to seek an annulment of his marriage and sue his wife for fraud. Rhinelander claimed that his wife, Alice, had concealed the fact that she was "colored." Alice denied the charge, arguing that her mixed racial origins were obvious, and she had never claimed to be white. Although the jury eventually came down in Alice's favour, the trial was a humiliating ordeal. At one point in the proceedings, Alice was made to partially undress so that the jury could get a closer look at her skin tone.

THE PASSING GENRE

The USA's preoccupation with 'passing' in the late nineteenth and early twentieth centuries was reflected in a literary genre devoted to the subject. A whole range of novelists created black characters who passed as white.

Some of the first passing novels featured male protagonists. Mark Twain's *Pudd'nhead Wilson* (1894), for example, follows the lives of two boys—one is white, the other has black ancestry. The boys look similar and are swapped as babies. The white boy becomes a slave, and his black lookalike becomes master of the house. Both boys are shown to adapt well to their roles, highlighting the arbitrary nature of the 'colour line.'

The Tragic Mulatta

As the passing genre developed, novelists more commonly chose young women as their protagonists. These mixed-race characters are attracted by the idea of a life with all the benefits of "whiteness." Inevitably, however, the characters' attempts to pass as white are exposed, often as a result of falling in love. This is the scenario in Charles W. Chesnutt's novel *The House Behind the Cedars* (1900). After learning that her brother has passed as a white man for years, the protagonist, Rena Walden, embarks on life as a white woman. All goes well until she falls in love with George Tryon, a white aristocrat. Just before they marry, George discovers the truth about Rena's identity and calls the marriage off. George comes to regret his decision, but Rena dies before the couple can be reunited.

Rena Walden's tragic fate was echoed in a host of other novels about young women who pass. In Vara Caspary's 1929 novel *The White Girl*, Solaria successfully lives as a white woman until her darker-skinned brother appears, blowing her cover. After her true identity is revealed, she commits suicide by drinking poison. Meanwhile, in Geoffrey Barnes's *Dark Lustre* (1932), the passing protagonist, Alpine, dies in childbirth.

As characters, Rena, Solaria and Alpine all fulfilled the popular literary stereotype of the "tragic mulatta." The tragic mulatta is a light-skinned woman of mixed racial heritage who feels estranged from both black and white society. Her decision to fraudulently pass as white is eventually punished—usually by exposure of her secret and untimely death.

In her 1933 novel *Imitation of Life*, Fannie Hurst offered a slightly different slant to the tragic mulatta's trajectory. In this story, a character called Peola successfully passes and marries a white man. To do so, however, she cuts all ties with her family, effectively breaking her mother's heart. When her mother dies at the end of the novel, Peola is wracked by remorse and grief. Her punishment for passing is alienation from her family and guilt over her mother's death. The novel was adapted twice for Hollywood, in 1933 and 1959. Both movies made much of the melodramatic potential of the passing genre.

Passing by Nella Larsen

The most famous example of the passing novel is Nella Larsen's *Passing*, first published in 1929. Like Charles W. Chesnutt, Larsen was biracial, so had considerable insight into why a person might try to 'pass.' Her novel was written at a time when passing was a topic of hot debate.

Larsen's novel focuses on two childhood friends: Clare Kendry and Irene Redfield. Both women are of mixed racial heritage. Irene has a husband and two sons and lives in Harlem. Clare, meanwhile, has been passing as white for years. She has a daughter by her rich, white husband, Jack Bellew.

When Clare gets in touch with her again, Irene senses that her old friend is trouble. Nevertheless, she ends up embroiled in Clare's life. Despite being married to a racist, Clare behaves recklessly, exposing herself to discovery. She introduces Jack to Irene, encouraging him to believe that she is white. As a result, Jack makes racist comments in front of Irene, and she is forced to go along with the charade to protect Clare.

Becoming increasingly careless, Clare frequents Harlem on a regular basis and mixes with other people of colour. She is finally caught out when Jack discovers that Irene is biracial, and by association, realises his wife must be too. Irene fails to warn Clare of Jack's discovery, as she suspects her friend is having an affair with her husband. At the end of the novel, Jack confronts Clare at a party also attended by Irene. During the confrontation, Clare is standing by the window and somehow plummets to her death. The cause of Clare's fall remains ambiguous. It may have been suicide, but it is also possible that Irene pushed her.

Larsen's novel conveys mixed messages about the ethics of passing. Readers can understand why Clare pretends to be white as the role affords her status, wealth and freedom. Refusing to conform to the stereotypical "tragic mulatta," she feels no sense of alienation or remorse. In fact, by socialising freely with black friends, Clare defies her husband and white society in general. At the same time, however, she must endure the racist comments of her husband without complaint.

In the end, Clare's reckless behaviour courts disaster. Despite her spirited personality, she suffers a tragic fate when she falls to her death. Her deception is exposed, and she pays the ultimate price for 'passing.'

Passing in *The Vanishing Half*

In *The Vanishing Half*, Bret Bennett engages with many of the tropes of passing fiction. She uses and develops some of the literary conventions while subverting others. The result is a take on passing which feels both classic and contemporary.

As in Nella Larsen's *Passing*, the novel focuses on two black women who look white. While Larsen chose childhood friends as her protagonists, Bennett intensifies the similarities between her characters by making them identical twins. Starting from the same origins, Desiree and Stella follow diverging paths.

Stella's decision to become white enables her to marry a rich, white man and have a daughter with him—just like Clare in *Passing*. Stella's husband, Blake, however, has little in common with the crass bigot, Jack Bellew. Blake is not knowingly racist and even feels embarrassed when Stella expresses openly bigoted views. He is white and privileged, however, and views African Americans as a separate, inferior species. As a result, Bennett's investigation of the role race plays in the marriage is much more nuanced.

Stella also diverges from Clare in attitude and behaviour. Where Clare is reckless, Stella's entire existence revolves around keeping the secret of her racial identity. Everything about her is guarded. Like Peola in *Imitation of Life*, she limits the risk of discovery by cutting all ties with her family.

Bennett draws a clear parallel with Larsen's *Passing* when she describes Stella leaning out of a window to smoke at a party. However, Stella is not to face the same tragic end as Clare. She continues to keep her race a secret from her husband and is never 'punished' for her actions. Instead, Stella suffers in more subtle ways. Always anxious, she can never be her true self. While she feels an imposter in the white community, she must keep herself apart from the people she instinctively wants to be with (her family and Loretta Walker).

Although alienation is the price Stella pays for passing, she chooses to maintain the pretence. Despite her inner conflict, she remains committed to the path she has taken. Her decision deeply wounds her mother and sister, but nobody dies of a broken heart. There is no melodrama here—just an empathetic assessment of the costs on all sides.

The Vanishing Half also investigates the inherent paradox of passing. On one level, pretending to be white can be seen as an act of defiance. After all, what could better highlight the arbitrary nature of discrimination based on skin colour? The ease with which Stella steps into the life of a white woman exposes the tenuous nature of binary racial categories. Simply by "playing white," she has instant access to advantages that would be barred to her as a black woman. Through the act of passing, Stella fools white society and refuses to accept her allocated 'place' in the pecking order.

At the same time, Stella's passing is shown to involve significant personal cost: namely the loss of an authentic sense of identity. The nature of passing also means that society never discovers just what Stella has got away with, so cannot appreciate its transgressive implications. By blending into white society, and accepting the privileges that come with it, Stella ultimately reinforces the racial status quo.

Readers may have their own ideas about whether Stella's

decision to pass is right or wrong. The author, however, deliberately avoids passing moral judgment on Stella. Instead, Bennett encourages readers to think about the kind of society that would induce a person to make this decision in the first place. Ultimately, all Stella wants is the same life opportunities as a white person. The fact that she must commit to a life of deceit to achieve this speaks volumes about the injustices of racial discrimination.

STYLE

The Vanishing Half is a family saga spanning three generations. An omniscient third-person narrator conveys the viewpoints of the novel's varied cast. Readers are given insight into the thoughts of characters like Early and Adele, as well as the four protagonists: Desiree, Stella, Jude, and Kennedy.

By interweaving the perspectives of Desiree and Stella with those of their daughters, the author traces the different ways their family history has influenced these characters. Each perspective is conveyed with compassion and a lack of moral judgment.

As well as flitting from character to character, the narrative shifts back and forth in time. The story covers four decades, from the 1950s to the 1990s. It skips from one time period to another, sometimes within the space of a single chapter. Bennett chooses this non-linear timeframe to emphasise the repercussions of her characters' decisions. Choices made by Desiree and Stella years earlier are shown to have an impact years down the line, for their daughters as well as themselves. Stella's decision to turn her back on her past and become white produces a daughter who is materially advantaged but lost. Meanwhile, Desiree's decision to return to the colourist town of Mallard has a lasting impact on Jude's sense of self-esteem.

PLOT SYNOPSIS

Part 1: The Lost Twins (1968)

<u>Chapter 1</u>

The novel opens in 1968 in Mallard, Louisiana. Mallard is a small town where light-skinned African Americans have intermarried for generations. The inhabitants are proud of their lightness, and most of them could be mistaken for white.

In the local diner (Lou's Egg House), Lou LeBon shares scandalous news. He tells his customers that one of the Vignes twins has returned to Mallard—accompanied by a dark-skinned daughter. The twins have not been seen since 1954 when they ran away as sixteen years old.

When she was a girl, Desiree Vignes disliked Mallard's colourist attitude to dark skin and longed to escape. Meanwhile, her studious twin sister, Stella, dreamed of becoming a teacher in their hometown. At the end of tenth grade, the twins were taken out of school and sent to clean for the Duponts—a rich, white family. Unbeknown to her sister, Stella was sexually assaulted by Mr Dupont. On Founder's Day, Desiree suggested leaving for New Orleans. Stella agreed, and the twins ran away that night.

Before returning to Mallard, Desiree lived in Washington, D.C. with her husband Sam and her daughter Jude. Sam—a black attorney—had become increasingly abusive during the marriage. When her husband throttled her and threatened her with a gun, Desiree decided to leave. She and Jude fled their apartment in the middle of the night.

In New Orleans, a bounty hunter, Early Jones, takes on a new job. He agrees to search for a woman who has disappeared with a client's child. When he is shown a photograph of the missing woman, Early recognises her as Desiree Vignes. When he was sixteen, Early worked on a farm in Mallard and had a crush on Desiree.

Chapter 2

When Desiree was a girl, her father was killed by a group of white men. She and her sister witnessed their father being dragged out of the house where he was shot. Leon Vignes survived the first attack, but the men returned to the hospital where he was recovering, shooting him in the head.

Desiree and Jude seek refuge with Desiree's mother, Adele. Adele has never seen her granddaughter before and is disapproving of Jude's dark skin. Nevertheless, she persuades them to stay in Mallard. Jude registers for school and Desiree travels to Opelousas to apply for a job in the sheriff's office. Desiree has worked as a fingerprint examiner for the federal government, and the sheriff's deputy is initially impressed by her credentials. When he sees she lives in Mallard, however, he realises that Desiree is black and sends her away.

Desiree goes to Mallard's bar, the Surly Goat. She sees Early Jones and remembers flirting with him as a 16-year-old. They talk, and Early pulls off Desiree's scarf, revealing the bruises Sam left on her neck. Angry, Desiree pushes him away and leaves the bar.

Chapter 3

In Mallard, Desiree takes a job waiting tables at Lou's Egg House. Early tells Desiree what he does for a living and admits that he was working for her husband, Sam. He calls Sam and says that he is unable to find Desiree. Early then offers to help Desiree find her missing twin, Stella. He leaves

Mallard to carry out a job in Texas but calls Desiree at the diner every day.

Early returns and takes Desiree to New Orleans to look for Stella. When the sixteen-year-old twins first arrived in New Orleans, they worked in a laundry together. Desiree then encouraged Stella to apply for a better paid secretarial job at the Maison Blanche department store. Pretending to be white, Stella got the job. A year later, she left with no warning, leaving a note of apology for Desiree.

Early and Desiree speak to Farrah Thibodeaux—the girl with whom the twins used to share an apartment. Farrah says she once saw Stella walking arm in arm with a white man. When Stella recognised Farrah, she pretended not to see her.

Desiree goes to Maison Blanche and acts white to gain entry to the offices. She discovers that Stella's last known contact address was in Boston, Massachusetts.

Early and Desiree return to Mallard and begin a relationship.

Part II: Maps (1978)

<u>Chapter 4</u>

Desiree has been back in Mallard for ten years. Early still visits her frequently, staying with her whenever he can. Despite his talents as a people hunter, he has been unable to track Stella's movements beyond Boston.

Jude has earned a scholarship at UCLA and arrives in Los Angeles. She meets Reese Carter—a handsome young black man—at a party.

<u>Chapter 5</u>

Jude and Reese become inseparable. As their friendship deepens, he reveals that he was born Therese Anne Carter. Jude moves into Reese's apartment, but their relationship remains platonic.

One day Jude returns to the apartment and catches Reese with his shirt off. She sees that his chest is bandaged and surrounded by bruising. Jude tells Reese that he should not bandage his chest if it causes him pain. She tries to reassure him that she does not care how he looks, but Reese is angry and defensive. Later Reese apologises and explains he is saving up for illegal surgery. They become lovers.

Chapter 6

Jude wants to pay for Reese's surgery and begins working for a catering company in her spare time. Sent to serve drinks at a party in Beverley Hills, she talks to one of the guests—a wealthy white girl with striking, violet eyes. The white girl's mother arrives late to the party. When Jude sees her, she drops the bottle of red wine she is holding.

Part III: Heartlines (1968)

Chapter 7

In Brentwood—an affluent area of Los Angeles—the residents of the Palace Estates hold an emergency meeting. The President of the Homeowners' Association announces that an African American family are attempting to buy one of the houses on the estate. The announcement causes indignation and uproar. Stella Sanders—an ordinarily quiet woman—stands up in the meeting and declares that they must be stopped.

Stella now lives a life of comfort and privilege. She met her husband Blake when she was his secretary in New Orleans and has been married to him for eight years. Their seven-year-old daughter Kennedy has fair hair, pale skin and violet eyes. Blake and Kennedy both believe that Stella is white.

After threatening legal action, the African American family move into the house opposite Stella's. Stella is terrified that they will recognise her as an imposter.

Chapter 8

Stella's new neighbours turn out to be Reginald and Loretta Walker. Reginald is an actor who plays a police officer on a popular TV drama.

One day Stella sees Kennedy playing with Cindy (the Walkers' daughter) in the street. Rushing outside, she drags Kennedy away. Stella justifies her actions by telling Kennedy "we don't play with niggers" (a phrase she once heard as a child). Later that day, Loretta Walker comes over with the doll abandoned by Kennedy in the street. She hands the doll to Stella without a word.

Stella bakes a cake as an apology to Loretta. The two women become friends, and their daughters regularly play together. Stella feels more at ease with Loretta than with any of the other women in the neighbourhood. Nevertheless, she tries to avoid being seen calling on her. She instructs Kennedy not to tell Blake about her playdates with Cindy.

One day Loretta invites Stella to join her whist group. Loretta's black friends voice their disapproval of the Walkers' determination to send Cindy to the all-white Brentwood Academy. When the women argue that Cindy will be miserable at the school, Stella agrees, confirming that many of her neighbours are opposed to it. Loretta's friends suggest that Stella should defend the Walkers against their white critics in the neighbourhood.

Chapter 9

Stella regularly lies to Blake about where she has been after seeing Loretta. The friendship between the two women has become the subject of gossip in the Estates.

On Christmas Eve, the Sanders throw a party for the neighbours, but Stella does not invite the Walkers. When one of the guests refers to Stella's friendship with Loretta, Stella denies it. She loses her temper when another guest observes that Stella has been seen calling on Loretta. Storming out of the room, she declares it is none of their business.

On Christmas Day, Kennedy and Cindy play outside together. When both girls begin crying, Stella goes out to investigate. During a squabble, Kennedy has upset Cindy by saying that she does not "want to play with a nigger." Loretta is furious when she learns what has happened and tells Stella to stay away from her. At home, Stella slaps Kennedy. She then kisses her daughter to apologise.

At a sewing circle, Stella lies to the other women, claiming that Reginald Walker looks at her in a way that makes her feel uncomfortable. A few days later, a brick is thrown through the Walkers' living-room window. The same thing happens a few days later, and this time, Cindy is injured by the broken glass. By March, the Walker family have moved out of the area.

Part IV: The Stage Door (1982)

<u>Chapter 10</u>

Jude and Reese share a cramped apartment in Koreatown. Jude works in a restaurant while studying to go to medical school. Reese has a job at the Kodak store.

After dropping the bottle of red wine at the Beverly Hills party, Jude lost her catering job. Since glimpsing Stella, she has thought about her aunt a great deal. She did not tell her mother about the sighting.

When their friend Barry lands a place in the chorus line, Jude and Reese go to see a musical in downtown Los Angeles. A young blonde woman is cast in the lead role, and Jude recognises her as the girl with violet eyes from the Beverly Hills party. From the playbill, Jude discovers the girl's name is Kennedy Sanders.

Jude goes to the matinee performance of the show the next day and bumps into Kennedy outside. Kennedy asks

Jude to help her get into her costume. Jude takes the opportunity to question Kennedy about her background. She learns that Kennedy's mother was born Stella Vignes and grew up in Louisiana.

Chapter 11

After the Walkers left her neighbourhood, Stella sank into a depression. Deciding to go back to school, she took a bachelor's degree in statistics. She now works in the mathematics department at Santa Monica College. Her new career causes tension with Blake, who wants her to be at home.

Kennedy has dropped out of college to pursue an acting career. Stella takes her daughter to lunch and unsuccessfully tries to persuade her to return to college.

Chapter 12

Jude takes a weekend job at the theatre. She pumps Kennedy for information about Stella whenever the opportunity arises. To Jude's disappointment, Stella never comes to watch the shows.

Chapter 13

On closing night, Stella finally turns up to watch her daughter perform. When Stella goes out for a cigarette, Jude follows. Jude tells Stella that she is from Mallard and her mother is Desiree Vignes. Stella does not believe Jude and demands to know who she really is. Jude tells Stella that Desiree returned to Mallard and has spent years trying to find her. Stella insists that she cannot return to her old life and hurries away.

At the after-show party, Kennedy comments on Reese's good looks. In doing so, she implies that a dark-skinned woman like Jude is lucky to be with such a handsome man. Angry, Jude informs Kennedy that their mothers are twin sisters.

Kennedy tells her mother about Jude. Stella denies everything, claiming to have never even heard of Mallard. Afraid that her husband will hear about it, Stella tells Blake that a black girl is falsely claiming to be Kennedy's cousin.

Part V: Pacific Cove (1985/1988)

Chapter 14

Kennedy dwells on Jude's claims while Stella continues to deny everything. Although Kennedy finds it improbable that she is related to Jude, she knows that Stella is secretive about her past. She also remembers her mother saying, years earlier, that she came from a small town called Mallard.

By 1985, Kennedy is living in a New York apartment with her black boyfriend, Frantz. Stella makes it clear that she disapproves of the relationship.

Kennedy lands a role in a musical and works in a coffee shop by day. Jude and Reese are also in New York, as Reese has travelled there for chest surgery. By chance, Jude spots Kennedy in the café and approaches her. Kennedy is reluctant to speak to Jude but is intrigued when Jude says she has something she wants to show her. They agree to meet at the theatre after Kennedy's show that night.

Chapter 15

After her performance, Kennedy finds Jude, Reese and Frantz waiting in the lobby for her. They go to a bar and Jude gives Kennedy a photo of Desiree and Stella as girls. Kennedy does not comment on the picture and makes an excuse to go home early.

Kennedy's curiosity gets the better of her, and she intercepts Jude at the hospital where Reese is having surgery. Jude reveals that the photograph of the twins was taken at a funeral. She explains to Kennedy that white men murdered their mothers' father, and the twins witnessed this attack. Kennedy visits her mother and confronts her with the photograph. Stella denies that the girl in the photograph is her.

Kennedy leaves Frantz and travels aimlessly for a year. As she tries to "find" herself, she makes up various stories about her background and identity.

By 1988, Kennedy has secured a regular acting job on a soap opera. Her role as girl-next-door Charity Harris comes to an end when she is written out of the show.

By the early 1990s, Kennedy is in her thirties and struggles to get acting work. In 1996 she goes to realty school. Securing a job with a real estate company, she shows houses to clients.

Part VI: Places (1986)

<u>Chapter 16</u>

Stella has not heard from Kennedy since their confrontation over the photograph. Fearing that Jude has caused a permanent rift with her daughter, she becomes desperate and decides to travel to Mallard. Stella hopes that Desiree can persuade Jude never to contact Kennedy again. On the journey, Stella is surprised to learn that Mallard no longer exists. The town's lines were redrawn in 1980, and it has become Palmetto.

Having worked at Lou's diner for many years, Desiree is now the manager. She feels tied to the twin responsibilities of running the diner and caring for her mother, who has Alzheimer's.

Desiree and Early are still a couple, and Early takes care of Adele when Desiree is working. He has abandoned bounty hunting for a regular job at the oil refinery. One day Early takes Adele fishing, and when they return home, they see a woman sitting on the porch. Early mistakes the stranger for a white woman, but Adele immediately recognises her as Stella. She greets her daughter as if she has never been away. Early suggests that Stella should fetch Desiree.

Desiree is angry when Stella first walks into the diner. Stella begs for forgiveness, and they finally embrace. That evening, after dinner, the twins sit on the porch and talk. Stella tells Desiree how Jude found Kennedy and exposed her secret. She asks Desiree to intervene with Jude on her behalf.

The next morning Early catches Stella sneaking out of the door. She tells him she must return to her life but, if she has to say goodbye, will not be able to do it. Early drives Stella to the train station. Before she leaves, Stella gives Early her diamond wedding ring and tells him to sell it to look after her mother. Desiree wakes up to find Stella has gone from the bed they shared as girls.

A month later, Kennedy contacts her parents to say she is moving back to California. Stella picks Kennedy up from the airport, and her daughter immediately notices her missing wedding ring. Stella admits that she gave it to her sister and invites Kennedy to ask anything about her past. The only condition she imposes is that Kennedy must keep what she learns a secret from Blake.

Chapter 17

At medical school, Jude learns that Adele has died. She calls Kennedy to share the news about their grandmother. Unbeknown to their mothers, Jude and Kennedy remain in regular touch with each other.

Leading up to Adele's death, Desiree continued to take care of her mother. Towards the end of her life, Adele continually referred to Desiree as Stella, as if she only remembered having one daughter. After the funeral, Desiree and Early start a new life together. They move to Houston where Desiree takes a job in a call centre.

Jude returns to Mallard for her grandmother's funeral. After the ceremony, she and Reese go down to the river. Taking their clothes off, they wade in and float in the water.

SETTING

Mallard

The Vignes twins are raised in rural Louisiana in the small town of Mallard. Mallard is entirely populated by Creoles, but a passing stranger might easily mistake it for an all-white community. For several generations, light skin has been carefully cultivated in the town.

The paradoxically white community of African Americans was founded by Alphonse Decuir—the Vignes twins' great-great-great-grandfather. The son of a slave and her master, Decuir inherited sugarcane fields from his white father and used the land to establish Mallard. His vision was of a town where "[a] more perfect Negro" would be created.

Decuir's idea of perfection was that "[e]ach generation" would be "lighter than the one before." This result would be achieved through endogamy (the practice of only marrying within one's community). By the time Decuir's great-great-great-granddaughters are born, his plan has come to fruition. The Vignes twins boast the kind of creamy complexions dreamed of by their forefather.

On one level, the establishment of Mallard can be seen as a rebellion against the binary categories of black and white. By claiming an identity that is somewhere between the two, Mallardians highlight the inadequacy of rigid racial categories. This being said, there is something insidious in the town's attitude to skin tone.

The description of Mallard as "more idea than place," reflects the fact that it was built upon Decuir's notion of a "utopia." It also suggests that Bennett created the fictional town to represent a broader theme: namely the USA's history of colourism. The entire ethos of Mallard centres on the idea that whiteness is superior. Paler skin is equated with beauty, while those with darker skin tones are considered unattractive and inferior. This attitude embodies colourism: the prejudice against dark skin within black communities.

Bennett based the colourist society of Mallard on her mother's stories of Creole towns in Louisiana where pale skin was prized. The author was also influenced by the clubs and societies that emerged in the USA after slavery was abolished. From the nineteenth century onwards, groups of light-skinned African Americans formed "Blue Vein" Societies in many U.S. cities. Membership depended on a person's skin being light enough to show the blue veins underneath. This concept is referenced in *The Vanishing Half* when Stella remembers "[h]er father had been so light that, on a cold morning, she could turn his arm over to see the blue of his veins." A similar colourist practice was the "paper bag test." At the entrance of certain clubs, and even churches, admission would only be granted after a paper bag was held against their skin. Those who were darker than the bag would be turned away.

In *The Vanishing Half*, Bennett effectively conveys the colourism of Mallard by representing a community with one judgmental frame of mind. When Desiree returns with her "blueblack" daughter, the community's sensibilities are offended. The common consensus is that Desiree should be ashamed of her daughter's skin tone: "If nothing could be done about ugliness, you ought to at least look like you were trying to hide it." The town instils such values into its children from an early age. As girls, Stella and Desiree are instructed to marry light and warned against the dubious intentions of dark boys.

Mallard's insular values are shown to have a lasting impact on how the characters view themselves and other people. The twins flee Mallard on Founder's Day in a symbolic rejection of everything it represents. Even after they escape, however, their feelings and decisions are shaped by the town. In an extension of Mallard's 'the paler, the better' attitude, Stella decides to 'become' white. Meanwhile, Desiree rails against her colourist indoctrination by marrying a dark-skinned man. When the marriage turns sour, however, Desiree retreats to Mallard. This means that her dark-skinned daughter bears the full brunt of the town's colourism while growing up there. Jude's formative years in Mallard leave her with the unshakable belief that her dark skin is repellent.

While Mallard's citizens are proud of their pale skin, Bennett points out that lightness is often "inherited at great cost." Alphonse Decuir's mother, for example, hated her son's light skin—presumably because it was a lasting reminder of rape or sexual coercion by her master. While some mixed-race relationships were consensual, many were not, and the shade of a child's skin was often a legacy of the horrors of slavery.

Outside of Mallard, the skin tone of the residents is shown to mean very little. They may be pale, but they are still black, meaning they are subject to the same prejudice and socio-economic disadvantages as other African Americans. Despite the visibility of his blue veins, Leon Vignes is murdered by a group of racist white men. His wife survives by taking in white people's laundry, and their daughters must give up school to clean for a white family—leaving Stella vulnerable to sexual assault. Lightness offers no benefits, except the empty satisfaction of feeling superior to darker-skinned people of colour.

Mallard is so small that it cannot be found on any map and, in 1980, it ceases to exist altogether. The parish redraws Mallard's geographic lines, and it becomes Palmetto. The town's erasure suggests that Mallard and its values have become obsolete following the progress made by the Civil Rights Movement. However, while the town is officially renamed, its citizens set little store by the revision. Changing a name is easy, but reshaping people's ideas is less so.

New Orleans

Desiree and Stella escape the restrictions of Mallard when they flee to New Orleans as sixteen-year-olds. While the city is more culturally diverse and offers the excitement of jazz clubs, life there does not turn out to be easy. Job opportunities are still limited for non-whites, and the twins must take whatever work they can get. Ironically, they end up working in a laundry—the kind of work they resented their mother having to perform in Mallard. Toiling for hours, they still struggle to pay the rent on even the shabbiest apartment.

Although Desiree was the sister most eager to leave Mallard, she is the one who feels homesick. Stella remains determined to stay in New Orleans to secure a better future. Eventually, Stella concludes that the only way to overcome the limits of segregation is through deceit. Passing as white, she secures a secretarial job at the department store, Maison Blanche.

Los Angeles

Stella, Blake and Kennedy live in Brentwood, Los Angeles. The upper-middle-class luxury of the Palace Estates contrasts sharply with the rusticity of Stella's hometown. Nevertheless, the gated community is shown to be just as insular.

The white residents of the Estates think of themselves as civilised and progressive. Some, like Blake, express sadness at the death of Martin Luther King Jr. However, the community's true feelings on civil rights are put to the test when a black family buys a house in the neighbourhood. An emergency Homeowners' Association meeting is immediately held, and every effort is made to prevent the Walker family from making the purchase. Bennett highlights the hypocrisy of the residents by pointing out that, despite their alleged support of Martin Luther King, "they still wouldn't have allowed the man to move into their neighborhood."

The racism the community displays towards the Walkers is

initially of a passive variety. While no one would dream of shouting racist insults, the African American family are socially ostracised. The bigotry becomes aggressive when Stella implies that Reginald Walker has improper designs on her. By invoking the stereotype of the black man as a sexual predator, Stella brings the community's racist fears and beliefs to the surface. Soon the residents are throwing bricks through the Walkers' window and leaving dog excrement on their lawn. The hate crimes, which eventually drive the Walkers out, bear a troubling similarity to the actions of the white mob who killed Stella's father in Louisiana.

When Jude goes to UCLA, she is shown to have a completely different experience of Los Angeles to her aunt. After being persecuted in Mallard, Jude experiences an unprecedented sense of freedom in L.A. She finds her own community in Reese and his friends who affirm that it is acceptable to be different.

California is shown to have different faces to different people. The privileged white suburbia of Brentwood could be a million miles away from the diversity Jude encounters in central Los Angeles. This point is underlined by the two contrasting embodiments of California in the novel. When Desiree glimpses a photo of Kennedy, the blonde girl's image seems to epitomise her idea of California. Jude, on the other hand, learns that the American state was originally named after a dark-skinned Amazonian queen.

CHARACTERS

Stella Vignes / Stella Sanders

Stella is the vanishing half of the novel's title. She is the twin who severs all ties with her sister and mother to pass as a white woman.

Stella's deliberate vanishing act is particularly difficult for her family to process, as it seems so out of character. As girls, she and her twin Desiree are presented as opposites, and Stella is the good sister: studious, reliable and dutiful. The extent of her dreams is to become a schoolteacher in Mallard.

As the story unfolds, we see that a series of events prompt Stella's life-changing decision. The first is her father's murder, which the twins partially witness as children. The brutal killing of Leon Vignes teaches Stella a hard lesson: lighter skin offers no protection from the violence and prejudice of white society. The second turning point for Stella comes when she and Desiree are taken out of school at the end of tenth grade. The termination of her education shatters Stella's hopes of becoming a teacher. The subsequent cleaning job for a wealthy, white family then leads to her sexual assault at the hands of Mr Dupont.

For Stella, working for the Duponts offers a steep learning curve. It clarifies the kind of treatment she can expect as a black woman (poorly paid work coupled with abuse). It also lays bare the economic advantages available to white folks. The Duponts' home is extravagantly luxurious, and Stella cannot help but imagine how it would feel to live in such a house. Desiree catches her twin imagining just that as Stella sits at her employer's vanity unit and stares "wistfully" into the mirror. With these contrasting lifestyles in mind, Stella agrees when Desiree suggests they should run away to New Orleans.

Another significant moment for Stella is the first time she is mistaken for a white girl. The experience makes her realise that this could be a credible disguise. Thus, when she later sees a 'whites-only' secretarial job advertised, she applies. At Maison Blanche, she takes on the persona of Miss Vignes or "White Stella." At this point, her identity starts to fracture. Stella begins to think of Miss Vignes as a separate person who leads a more desirable life.

When Stella's boss, Blake Sanders, shows romantic interest and asks her to move to Boston with him, she grasps the opportunity. Showing a surprising streak of independence, as well as a gift for deceit, Stella tells Desiree nothing and executes her escape perfectly. Her transition from a life of poverty to one of comfort and luxury as Blake's white wife appears effortless.

By committing herself to a life of passing, Stella gains many things. Whiteness brings her wealth and social status. More importantly still, it offers safety from the kind of bigotry that killed her father. It is easy to see why she convinces herself that pretending to be white is not only the best option but really the only one that makes sense. In choosing the advantages of being white, Stella provides a damning reminder of the disadvantages black Americans face in almost every area of their lives.

At first, Stella feels thrilled by her ability to fool white society and experience its freedoms. Over time, however, Bennett illustrates how passing takes its toll on her. To maintain her disguise as a white woman, she cuts all ties with her sister and mother. Although she creates a new family, she can never reveal her true self to her husband or daughter. The price of passing is shown to be loneliness and a lack of intimacy with others.

Aware of being an imposter, Stella lives with the perpetual dread of being caught out. Her greatest fear is that people of her racial background will immediately see through her disguise. For this reason, she avoids African Americans altogether. When a black family threaten to move into the neighbourhood, Stella's reaction is extreme. Usually reluctant to draw attention to herself, she stands up at the emergency residents' meeting and declares that the Walkers must not be permitted to live there. More shocking still is her behaviour when she first sees Kennedy playing in the street with the Walkers' daughter. Dragging Kennedy away, Stella declares that "we don't play with niggers."

In portraying Stella's racist conduct, Bennett suggests a complex mixture of motivations. Stella fears the Walkers as she worries that they will expose her identity. Publicly expressing hostility to their arrival also allows her to highlight her 'whiteness' to the rest of the community. In her response to her daughter playing with Cindy, Stella again shows an eagerness to identify herself as white. She aims to convince Kennedy that they have nothing in common with the black family over the road. We see her using a similar distancing strategy in her attitude to Jude, who she continually refers to as "That dark girl." By labelling her niece solely by her skin tone, she implies that they cannot possibly be related.

By allying herself so vehemently with the white perspective, Stella reinforces racial discrimination and white supremacy. She even outdoes the prejudiced behaviour of the other residents of Brentwood by resorting to the n-word. Miscalculating the more civilised brand of racism acceptable amongst the educated middle-classes, Stella mimics the more overt bigotry prevalent in the rural South. In fact, her racist tirade is a word-for-word repetition of something she heard as a child. A white girl's mother used the phrase as she dragged her daughter away from Stella and Desiree. Having been the target of this comment as a young black girl makes Stella's willingness to repeat it profoundly disturbing. Her actions suggest that she has internalised her role as a white woman so thoroughly that, for a moment, she believes her own rhetoric.

While the Walkers remain in Brentwood, their presence is a constant source of anxiety to Stella. At the same time, she feels drawn to Loretta Walker, who reminds her of Desiree and the roots she left behind. Stella feels a connection with Loretta that is lacking in her relationships with the white women of the community. She even fantasises about revealing her secret to Loretta. However, the friendship comes to an abrupt end when Stella's earlier racist comments come back to haunt her. When Kennedy calls Cindy a "nigger," Loretta guesses that the child has learned the word from her mother.

Shunned by Loretta, Stella comes up with a strategy to make the Walkers leave the neighbourhood for good. She tells the other wives that Reginald looks at her in a way that makes her "uncomfortable." As a black woman, she well knows the reaction her lie will cause. Within days, the Walkers have become the target of hate crimes, as their neighbours throw bricks through their windows at night. With a few well-chosen words, Stella places the Walkers in a situation akin to the most traumatic event of her own childhood. Of all Stella's actions, this is perhaps the most shocking.

Despite the many drawbacks of passing, Stella never once considers reverting to her authentic identity. Even when Kennedy confronts her mother with a photograph of the twins as children, she continues to deny her past. It is only at the point when Stella fears she will alienate Kennedy for good that she finally admits the truth. The confession offers a glimmer of hope for Stella's future relationship with her daughter. Her husband, however, remains ignorant of who she is. After a brief return to Mallard, Stella also resigns herself to never seeing her sister and mother again.

Stella's character is no tragic victim. Throughout the novel, she retains a sense of agency and, despite the compromises involved, remains convinced that she has made the right choices. Towards the conclusion of the story, we also see her fulfil her intellectual potential by returning to study and becoming a professor of statistics. As the threat of exposure passes, it seems likely that Stella will live life as a white woman to the end of her days. Readers are left to ponder whether, in her shoes, they would have done the same.

Desiree Vignes

As a girl, Desiree is restless and rebellious. Stifled by the claustrophobic atmosphere of Mallard, she rails against her community's obsession with lightness. Her childhood is spent longing to leave her hometown.

Desiree initially thinks of herself as the spirited, ambitious twin. She is the one who suggests escaping to New Orleans, and Stella follows her lead. However, Desiree realises that she has underestimated Stella when her sister breaks away to lead an entirely different life. Abandoned and hurt, Desiree spends the rest of her life mourning the absence of her sister.

While Stella embarks on a life as a white woman, Desiree takes the opposite trajectory. Rebelling against Mallard's rule of marrying light, she falls in love with a dark-skinned attorney, Sam. When their daughter Jude is born as dark as her father, Desiree is pleased.

When Sam becomes increasingly violent, Desiree realises that she and Jude must escape. Ironically, her instinct is to return to the hometown she left so eagerly. Despite her ambivalent feelings about Mallard, Desiree surprises herself by staying there for twenty years. After the unpredictable violence of her marriage, she finds comfort in returning to her roots.

Desiree essentially goes on to lead the life that she was desperate to avoid as a child. Stuck in Mallard, she suffers the social and economic disadvantages experienced by many black women. As Stella floats in her L.A. swimming pool drinking gin, Desiree works long hours as a waitress to make ends meet. Once Jude leaves home, her maternal duties are swiftly replaced by caring for her mother, who develops Alzheimer's disease.

On paper, Stella is the twin who gains all the advantages by passing. Desiree, who stays true to her roots, misses out. By giving readers access to the characters' inner lives, however, Bennett demonstrates that Desiree is the more contented of the sisters. An accepted member of Mallard's community, she, nevertheless, lives by her own rules. Refusing to feel shame at the shade of her daughter's skin, Desiree goes on to settle down with her dark-skinned lover, Early. Her life is hard, but her relationships with those around her are authentic.

After spending so many years back in her hometown, Desiree struggles to imagine a life beyond Mallard. When her mother dies, however, she decides to move to Houston with Early. There, she takes on a new lease of life, working at a call centre where she is known as Mama D. Readers are left with the sense that Desiree's life may have been 'smaller' than Stella's, but it has been one well-lived.

Jude Winston

Desiree's daughter Jude has a traumatic start in life. As a small child, she witnesses her father attacking her mother. Then, when Desiree decides to leave, Jude is uprooted from her home in Washington D.C. Suddenly she and her mother live in the backwater of Mallard with a grandmother she has only just met.

The move to Mallard is particularly challenging for Jude because of the colour of her skin. Amongst the uniformly "beige" children of the small town, Jude's dark skin tone stands out like a sore thumb. The residents are both transfixed and horrified by how dark she is. Desiree urges her daughter to ignore this prejudice, but Jude does not possess her mother's resilience. Quiet and studious, she is more like her aunt, Stella.

Spending her formative years in Mallard has a disastrous impact on Jude's self-image. Ostracised and verbally abused by other children, she comes to accept that her dark skin is ugly. Her sense of conflict over her appearance is exacerbated by the knowledge that she looks like her violent father. As a result, she feels lonely and that she does not really belong to anyone.

In the end, Jude transcends her circumstances through hard work and education. Pursuing her dream of going to medical school takes her to Los Angeles. In Reese and a community of drag queens, she finds a group of people who accept and celebrate difference. While Jude continues to struggle with self-esteem, she eventually accepts that Reese desires her. The fact that her boyfriend is so handsome is one in the eye for everyone who has told her that dark skin is unattractive.

Bennett chooses to end the novel with Jude bathing naked in Mallard's river with Reese. This image, with its baptismal connotations, reinforces the idea of overcoming trauma to become a new person. By concluding *The Vanishing Half* this way, the author suggests a hopeful future for Jude.

Kennedy Sanders

When Stella first sees her baby girl, she is overwhelmed with relief. Kennedy's blonde hair, pale skin and startlingly violet eyes do not even hint at her mother's true racial background. The epitome of the spoiled, rich, white girl, Kennedy is raised with all the social advantages that Jude lacks.

Stella hopes that Kennedy will live the kind of life she dreamed of as a girl. However, in planning her child's future, Stella overlooks the fact that Kennedy is nothing like her. Lacking Stella's studious and cautious nature, Kennedy is wild and hedonistic—more like her aunt, Desiree. Stella is resentful of the opportunities Kennedy squanders. She despairs of her daughter as she cuts high school classes, dates unsuitable boys, and drops out of college.

While Kennedy possesses all the material advantages, she suffers from a lack of groundedness. Hurt by her mother's continual evasions, she feels that Stella does not want to be known. When she encounters Jude, Kennedy is provided with answers to some of the mysteries surrounding her mother's identity. In order to fully accept Jude's claims, however, Kennedy must completely overhaul her already fragile sense of self.

In order to believe Jude's version of events, Kennedy must accept that her mother is African American and that she is biracial. Hampered by the notion that race can be easily visually identified, she struggles to reconcile her physical appearance with her heritage. Over several years, Kennedy swings back and forth between believing Jude and finding the whole idea too absurd to be credible. She only achieves closure when Stella, after many denials, admits the truth.

Kennedy's lack of a stable sense of identity draws her to acting. Paradoxically, the only time she truly feels herself is when she plays other people. After several years of striving to become a serious theatrical actor, she lands a role in a soap opera. Playing "girl next door" Charity Harris, Kennedy eventually leaves the soap when her character is written out of the series. For many years, however, soap fans recognise her as Charity.

When Kennedy hits her thirties, she starts selling real estate as the acting roles dry up. She approaches the work as an acting job, adapting each performance to the client. Bennett leaves readers with the feeling that Kennedy will, to some extent, always be on stage.

Adele Vignes

Adele is the mother of Stella and Desiree. Before marrying her husband, she was a Decuir—a descendent of Mallard's founder. The Decuirs are the closest thing to aristocracy in the small town. Thus, when Adele chose to marry "a Vignes boy," she was perceived to be marrying down, even though her husband was light-skinned.

Adele's impressive ancestry counts for very little when white men murder her husband. Struggling to make ends meet, she takes in white people's laundry and cleans for them. Financial necessity also means limiting the prospects of her daughters. When the twins finish tenth grade, Adele takes them out of school to start work as cleaners. This decision has momentous effects that Adele could not have anticipated. Stella's sexual assault at the hands of her employer leads to both twins fleeing Mallard at the age of sixteen.

Adele is a formidable character, not given to outward displays of emotion. When Desiree returns after fourteen years' absence, Adele is prickly with her daughter and expresses disapproval of her granddaughter's dark skin. Nevertheless, she is privately overjoyed and determinedly embarks on a campaign to convince them to stay in Mallard.

As Adele develops Alzheimer's, she becomes confused about the identities of those around her. When Stella finally returns unannounced, however, her mother immediately recognises her, as if she has never been away. In the days before her death, Adele hurts Desiree's feelings by continually referring to her as Stella. The mistake shows that, despite her reticence on the subject, Stella's continued absence has been a profound source of grief to Adele.

Leon Vignes

Stella and Desiree's father dies before the novel begins. Nevertheless, the manner of his death plays a crucial role in shaping the twins.

Leon was killed when the girls were young by white men running a rival repair business. Hiding in the closet, Stella and Desiree witnessed their father being dragged from the house before his attack. Although he survived, the white men returned to shoot him in hospital.

Both of the twins are traumatised by their father's death. Stella takes away the message that being black is dangerous.

As a result, she longs for the safety that whiteness confers. To Desiree, Leon's death confirms the futility of Mallard's obsession with light skin. The fact that her father could have passed for white does not save him from being murdered.

Blake Sanders

Blake is Stella's boss at Maison Blanche, and he goes on to make her his wife. The epitome of white, male privilege, he is Yale-educated and comes from a wealthy banking family. The extent of Blake's affluence is not immediately apparent to Stella as he does not flaunt his money or wear flashy clothes. Only later does she realise that this very understatement is a sign of someone from old, established money.

Blake has no idea that Stella is black—a source of narrative tension in the novel. Bennett is too subtle a writer, however, to paint him as a monstrous bigot. Instead, she creates an ironic scenario where he feels "embarrassed" at Stella's apparent aversion to African Americans. At one point, he ruefully reflects that "in all the time he'd known her, she'd never spoken kindly of a Negro." Blake assumes that Stella's attitude springs from an unfortunate upbringing as Southern "white trash." He wants no part of uncouth Southern racism, as embodied in the Ku Klux Klan. Thus, when someone throws a brick through the Walkers' window, he declares, "This is Brentwood, not Mississippi."

While Blake disapproves of overt racism, he still believes in white supremacy as "the natural order of things." Blake has grown up in a well-mannered world where black people are treated civilly but are nevertheless considered inferior. Brought up by a black nanny, he reflects that she was "*practically* family" (my italics). We also learn that, as a boy, he favoured "an ugly black rag doll" called Jimbo. Blake's steadfast attachment to the black doll suggests a blindness to race. When he finds the doll in tatters, however, he is surprised to find that its cotton insides are not brown. Blake's childish expectation highlights his belief that the differences between black and white go deeper than skin colour.

Blake demonstrates his 'us and them' attitude to race when he and Stella watch news coverage of the Watts riots. When he says, "I'll never understand why they do that ... Destroy their own neighborhoods" he clearly articulates his belief that people of colour are essentially different. What is more, the comment suggests that there is something irredeemably savage about their nature. The implications are not lost on Stella, who secretly goes to cry in the powder room.

Blake also shows a patriarchal streak when he complains about Stella going to university. While he is happy for his wife to take some classes to keep her amused, he does not want her to have a career. As with most of the characters, however, Bennett allows readers to feel a glimmer of sympathy for Blake's situation. Due to Stella's secrecy, it is impossible for him to really know his wife, and her moods remain inexplicable to him. As he never discovers his wife's secret, readers can only guess at how he would react to it.

Sam Winston

Desiree falls in love with the black attorney, Sam Winston, when she is working as a fingerprint examiner in Washington, D.C. He becomes Desiree's husband and Jude's father.

Initially, the dark shade of Sam's skin is part of his allure. For Desiree, he encapsulates all the boys she was warned to keep away from while growing up in Mallard. She hopes that the relationship will flourish and disprove those colourist attitudes. As the marriage sours, however, it is Sam who repeatedly brings up the difference in their skin tones. He unfairly suggests that Desiree thinks herself superior because she is lighter than him. For a while, Desiree justifies Sam's behaviour by telling herself it is the consequence of living in a racist society. When his violence escalates, she is forced to confront the fact that he may end up killing her.

After Desiree flees her marital home with Jude, Sam employs a bounty hunter to retrieve his wife and daughter. By doing so, he unwittingly reunites Desiree with her first love, Early Jones.

Early Jones

Early Jones begins the novel as a wanderer with no familial or geographical roots. The tone of his life was set at the age of eight when his parents (who had too many children) passed him on to his aunt and uncle. From that point, Early learned not to get too attached to any one person or place. After a childhood spent sharecropping on farms, he went to prison for several years for stealing car parts.

Early is a bounty hunter and visits Mallard to locate Desiree on behalf of her husband, Sam. Coincidentally, he is already familiar with the small town, having once worked on a farm there. As a dark-skinned black youth, Early found himself on the wrong end of Mallard's colourism. He recalls being slapped by a man in church for putting his hand in holy water before the man's wife. He also remembers being shooed off by Adele Vignes when she caught him flirting with her daughter, Desiree.

After meeting Desiree again and seeing her bruised neck, Early quickly decides that he will not divulge her whereabouts to Sam. Instead, he begins a relationship with her. Early's peripatetic life continues, but he finds himself returning to Mallard again and again to see Desiree. This marks his first real attachment to a person or place.

Early's enduring love for Desiree transforms him from a wanderer to a committed family man. Although Desiree refuses to marry a second time, Early shows his commitment to her in every possible way. Taking a regular job at the oil refinery, he works around Desiree's shifts at the diner in order to care for his 'almost' mother-in-law. The loving bond he builds with Adele as he braids her hair and takes her fishing is one of the great joys of the novel. Through his relationship with the Vignes women, Early shows himself to be a loyal, reliable, and thoroughly decent man. His actions disprove Adele's earlier warning that dark-skinned boys "don't want nothin good."

Reese Carter

Born Therese Anne Carter, Reese is a transgender man. Throughout the novel, Bennett draws parallels between Reese's experiences and those of Stella. Like Stella, Reese cuts all ties with his family in the South to become someone else. Both characters are also shown to be retreating from violence. Stella wants to escape Mr Dupont's sexual assaults, as well as the memory of her father's murder. Reese, meanwhile, runs away from the brutal reaction of his father when he discovers his 'daughter' dressed in men's clothes and kissing a female school friend.

Significant differences also exist between Reese's decision to transition to another identity and Stella's. Stella abandons her old life to pretend to be something she is not. She looks the part (i.e. white), but the role does not reflect who she really is. Reese, on the other hand, is on a journey to become his true self (an identity which contradicts his physical appearance). By passing, Stella seeks safety, security and social advantages, while Reese's quest involves facing uncertainty and prejudice.

Arriving in L.A. as a naïve seventeen-year-old, Reese has not even heard of the term transgender. Nevertheless, he has a strong sense of who he is and that his body does not fit with his identity. The novel outlines the challenges of being a transgender man in the late 1970s as Reese scrapes together money to buy steroids off the street—initially resorting to selling sex services.

When Jude first meets and falls for Reese, she has no idea that he is transgender. However, when Reese reveals the truth, it does not alter her feelings. Jude's experiences in Mallard mean that she understands how it feels to want to be someone else and to be persecuted for who you are. Her love for him is not conditional upon gender. When they begin a sexual relationship, Reese is even more self-conscious about his body than Jude. Ashamed of his breasts (which he keeps bandaged until he can afford surgery), he does not allow Jude to undress him. Their partnership is a poignant coming together of two vulnerable, traumatised souls.

Like Jude, Reese is shown to overcome his issues with self-image to become the person he wants to be. By the end of the novel, he has become a freelance photographer. He has also had the longed-for chest surgery, so he finally feels his body matches his inner identity. No longer ashamed to be seen naked, Reese goes shirtless in even the most inclement of weather.

Reginald Walker

Reginald Walker is a famous black actor who plays Sergeant Tommy Taylor on a popular TV drama. When the residents of Brentwood try to prevent him from buying a house there, he forces the matter by threatening legal action.

When Reginald and his family move in, the white residents of the neighbourhood feel less threatened when they realise that he is a familiar TV personality. His fame somehow makes him less 'other.' Some of the residents, like Blake, even greet him with Sergeant Taylor's catchphrase "File that form!" The tide of opinion swiftly turns, however, when Stella claims that she does not like the way Reginald looks at her. Once again, he is perceived as a threat, and the family are driven out of their home.

Loretta Walker

Stella dreads the arrival of a black family in her neighbourhood and her relationship with Loretta Walker gets off to a bad start. Seeing Kennedy playing with the Walkers' daughter in the street, Stella drags her daughter away and tells her, "we don't play with niggers." Later that day, Loretta wordlessly hands back the doll that Kennedy left abandoned in the street.

Loretta shows a forgiving nature when she accepts a lopsided cake from Stella as an apology. The two women become friends, and their daughters play together. They also discover that they have more in common than they thought. Loretta, like Stella, dreamed of a life in academia but gave it up to support her husband's acting career.

Forthright and funny, Loretta reminds Stella of Desiree. Stella feels more at ease with her than with any of the white women in the neighbourhood. Nevertheless, she tries to conceal their friendship, like a dirty secret. Loretta brings the relationship to an end when Kennedy finally repeats Stella's shocking racial slur to Cindy.

Loretta is less enthusiastic about moving to Brentwood than her husband. It is Reginald who insists on going through with the purchase, even when the white residents protest. Loretta does, however, take a stance against the local all-white school, threatening to sue them if they do not approve her daughter's admission. Torn between standing up for their rights, and her daughter's happiness, Loretta eventually sends Cindy to a school where she is less likely to be persecuted.

The way that the Walkers fight for their right to equal privileges contrasts with Stella's 'if you can't beat them, join them' attitude to race. Bennett makes it clear, however, that if the Walkers were less wealthy, they would not be in a position to fight their corner at all.

Cindy Walker

Loretta's daughter, Cindy, becomes Kennedy's childhood friend. The friendship ends when Kennedy calls Cindy a "nigger" (repeating the words of her mother).

Barry

When Reese first arrives in Los Angeles, he has the good fortune to meet Barry. Barry immediately grasps what Reese cannot yet articulate: that he is transexual. Taking the younger man under his wing, he introduces Reese to other people who are like him.

Barry is one of several characters in the novel who lead double lives. A high school chemistry teacher by day, he becomes glamorous drag queen, Bianca, at night and weekends. Barry's attitude to his double identity is refreshingly untroubled. Unlike Stella, he retains a clear sense of whom he is playing at any given time, reflecting, "You could live a life this way, split. As long as you knew who was in charge."

Barry becomes a mutual friend to Reese and Jude. Over the years, they remain in touch. During the 1980s, Barry informs them of the many friends and acquaintances who died during the AIDS epidemic.

Frantz

Frantz is Kennedy's first black boyfriend. While they are together, they share a basement apartment in New York.

When Stella discovers her daughter is dating Frantz, she reacts like a racist white woman. Looking for a reason other than his skin colour to explain her horror, she declares him "uppity." Stella's reaction is ironic as Frantz (who teaches physics at Columbia) is Kennedy's first respectable boyfriend.

Stella suspects that Kennedy's interest in Frantz is connected to her doubts about her racial ancestry. As Stella points out, Kennedy has never dated "anyone like this before." Certainly, Kennedy is shown to use her relationship with Frantz to get in touch with the black roots she struggles to believe she possesses. At one point, she tells Frantz that she is "part black" to test how feasible this seems. Frantz thinks she is joking, leaving Kennedy to conclude that "[l]oving a black man only made her feel whiter than before."

Lou LeBon

Lou is the owner of the only diner in Mallard—Lou's Egg House. At the beginning of the novel, he spreads the word that Desiree has returned with a "blueblack" daughter. He goes on to give Desiree a job waitressing and, twenty years later, she takes over as manager of the diner.

The Duponts

Stella and Desiree become cleaners for the Dupont family when they are taken out of school. Mrs Dupont patronises the twins by commenting on how "pretty" and "light" they are. Meanwhile, Mr Dupont sexually assaults Stella. Stella never tells anyone about her ordeal. Her desire to escape the situation, however, prompts her to agree when Desiree suggests running away to New Orleans.

Farrah Thibodeaux

A peer of the Vignes twins, Farrah Thibodeaux does the unthinkable by fleeing Mallard for New Orleans. Her actions demonstrate that leaving Mallard is possible, and a year later, Stella and Desiree follow her lead. When they first arrive in New Orleans, the twins sleep on Farrah's floor.

Farrah eventually settles down and marries an alderman. When Desiree visits her, years later, Farrah reveals that she once saw Stella walking arm in arm with a white man.

Big Ceel

Big Ceel is a bail bondsman, loan shark, and Early's employer. He gives Early jobs searching for missing people and criminals on the run.

Shortly after ceasing to work for Big Ceel, Early finds out that his former employer was stabbed to death during a card game. He also discovers that Ceel's real name was Clifton

Lewis.

Lonnie Goudeau

Lonnie is the first child in Mallard to call Jude "Tar Baby." During their schooldays together, he continues to persecute her regarding her skin colour. Adele suggests that Lonnie might taunt Jude because he likes her. Jude, however, finds this impossible to believe. When Lonnie watches her on the running track, she imagines he is mocking her.

Lonnie's intentions become apparent when he grabs sixteen-year-old Jude outside a barn and kisses her. He continues to meet with her for sexual encounters, but only ever in the dark and in secret. During the daytime, he does not even acknowledge Jude.

Lonnie's actions demonstrate that he desires Jude, but, thanks to Mallard's colourist attitudes, is ashamed of that desire. Jude's lack of self-esteem is poignantly illustrated by the fact that she continues to meet Lonnie, flattered that he even wants to touch her.

Percy White

Percy White is the President of the Homeowners' Association in the luxurious neighbourhood of Brentwood. He is the first to warn his neighbours of the imminent arrival of a black family. Later, he also proudly admits to throwing a brick through the Walkers' living room window. Percy's surname underlines his obsession with maintaining an all-white community.

Peg Davis

Peg teaches number theory and is Stella's mentor at Santa Monica College. The only female professor in the department, she encourages Stella to take a master's and a PhD. She also lends Stella books by feminist authors and invites her to attend protests against sexism. Stella notes, however, that there are no black women in Peg's feminist group.

Pam Reed

A seasoned black actor, Pam Reed is routinely cast as a judge. The irony is not lost on Pam, who points out how different society would be if justice really were placed in the hands of black women.

Pam makes a guest appearance in the soap opera Kennedy stars in. Off set, the two women share an awkward exchange. Eager to make a good impression on Pam, Kennedy blurts out that her first childhood friend was black. Pam ironically responds, "Lucky her."

THEMES & SYMBOLS

Racism and Colourism

The Vanishing Half addresses the familiar theme of racism. In addition, the novel focuses upon a related but less talked about form of prejudice—that of colourism. Colourism is the discrimination against people of colour by other (lighter-skinned) people of colour. For more on the history of colourism, see 'Background to the Vanishing Half.'

The novel opens in 1968 at a racially charged point in the USA's history. In the aftermath of Martin Luther King Jr.'s assassination, there are riots, and the future of the civil rights movement seems uncertain. It is at this point that we are introduced to twin sisters, Desiree and Stella. Both are light-skinned black women, but Stella is passing as white.

Bennett highlights the injustices of racism in American society through the consequences of the opposing choices of the Vignes twins. By "playing white" Stella gains access to job opportunities that would be barred to her under segregation. As a result, she acquires a rich husband, a luxurious home and social status. She is also safe from racist insults and the kind of racially motivated violence that killed her father. Desiree, meanwhile, fulfils the socially prescribed role of a black woman. Despite dreams of escaping, she finds herself stuck in her hometown performing poorly paid work to keep a roof over her head.

By locating her characters in different areas of the USA, the author highlights the insidious nature of American racism. The racist mob mentality of the rural South, epitomised in the KKK, is illustrated by the horrific murder of Leon Vignes by a group of white men. The white citizens of Brentwood, California, meanwhile consider themselves above such barbaric acts. Their pretence of enlightenment, however, is shown to be just that when Stella suggests that Reginald Walker looks at her in a way that makes her feel uncomfortable. By evoking the age-old racist myth that black men are a sexual threat to white women, Stella exposes the true colours of the residents. Soon afterwards, they are throwing bricks through the Walkers' living-room window. By directing racist hatred towards the Walkers, Stella reduces the chances of becoming the target of it herself.

Bennett creates a geographical space that embodies the concept of colourism in the small town of Mallard. So obsessed are the residents with the light tone of their skin that they have developed the custom of endogamy (only marrying within their own community).

When Jude is brought to Mallard as a child, the full extent of the town's colourism is revealed. Faced with a dark-skinned young girl, Mallardians display horrified fascination. Lou's observation that Jude looks "Like she flown direct from Africa" glosses over the fact that they all share similar ancestry. The attitude of the townspeople bears similarities to Stella's position in "playing white." The more they dwell on their lightness, the more they lose sight of their roots. Unlike Stella, however, they gain no social or economic advantages by distinguishing themselves from darker-skinned black Americans. Their colourism simply reinforces racist ideology.

While Mallard is portrayed as an extreme example of colourism, its citizens' attitudes are shown to reflect those of wider society. When Desiree gives birth to Jude in Washington, D.C., for example, the attending black nurse expects her to be dismayed at the dark shade of her baby's skin. Meanwhile, when Kennedy observes to Jude, "Your men usually like the light girls, don't' they?" she expresses an uncomfortable truth.

Throughout the novel, colourism is represented as a form of internalised racism. Black Americans have been told for so long that whiteness equates to superiority and beauty that they have begun to believe it. Bennett implies that as long as colourism reinforces racist beliefs, there is little hope of change.

Identity

When Stella commits to living life as a white woman, she discards one identity and takes on another. Instead of allowing others to define who she is, she chooses to control how others will see her. Passing is a transgressive act but also involves a denial of the authentic self. As a result, Stella feels a sense of alienation from herself as well as from those around her.

In Stella's case, manipulating how she is seen involves projecting a different racial identity. She is motivated not by the inner conviction that she is white but by the workings of a racist society. In a world where black identity is perceived as essentially different and inferior to white identity, passing is the logical solution.

In the course of the novel, Bennett presents other characters whose identity is a source of conflict to them. Transgender Reese, for example, experiences a disconnect between the gender role assigned to him at birth and his sense of self. On his journey from El Dorado to Los Angeles, he transforms himself from Therese to Reese. The metamorphosis involves cutting his hair, donning men's clothes, bandaging his chest, and even taking on a more masculine gait. Unlike Stella, Reese feels more himself the more he leaves his old identity behind until, "By Tucson, it was Therese who felt like a costume." The idea of authentic self-expression through changing one's appearance is later echoed in the character of Barry. A high school chemistry teacher, Barry becomes Bianca in his drag act. The dual "roles" express different aspects of his personality.

Jude is a poignant example of how others can adversely shape a person's sense of identity. Growing up in the colourist town of Mallard, she comes to believe that her dark skin makes her ugly and unlovable. Unlike Reese and Barry, Jude has no way of radically changing her physical appearance. Resorting to methods alleged to lighten the skin, she finds them all ineffective. Her only option is to move to a place where her dark skin will not be perceived in such negative terms. In Los Angeles, she finds a more accepting community.

It is no accident that when Jude first meets Reese at a Halloween party, they are both in costume—Jude as a cat, Reese as a cowboy. While playing roles, these two vulnerable characters feel confident enough to approach each other. When they later become lovers, it is significantly during a blackout at a party. Darkness momentarily frees both Jude and Reese from the anxieties that surround their physical appearance.

Kennedy is another character who struggles with her sense of identity. On the surface, she possesses all the traits which equate with a charmed life: white, blonde, pretty, and wealthy. Nevertheless, Kennedy's sense of who she is remains extremely tenuous. When Stella asks her daughter, "Why can't you just be yourself?" Kennedy frankly responds, "Maybe I don't know who that is." This lack of rootedness is shown to be, at least in part, due to Stella's secrecy. For many years, Kennedy is denied access to her family history. When she finally discovers that she is biracial, the truth seems too preposterous to comprehend.

By detailing her characters' inner conflicts, Bennett emphasises the complex nature of identity. For some, denying their innate identity leads to a sense of alienation. For others, a constructed identity more authentically expresses who they are. Each individual's sense of self is as unique as the fingerprints analysed by Desiree.

Twins

Bennett expands on the theme of identity by creating twins as her central characters. As girls, Stella and Desiree feel as if they are each half of one identity. Their sense of oneness is emphasised when Stella cuts her finger and Desiree instinctively puts her sister's finger in her mouth. Both depend on the presence of the other for their sense of self.

Stella and Desiree's identities are shown to form in direct response to the traits the other twin possesses or lacks. Desiree is high-spirited and rebellious, so Stella becomes cautious and reliable. Desiree speaks out, while Stella takes refuge in silence. As they grow older, and these differences become more pronounced, the girls increasingly feel as if they are "two bodies poured into one, each pulling it her own way."

The contrast between the twins' characters eventually leads them to take completely different paths in life. When Stella deserts Desiree to pursue a life as a white woman, their lives split "as evenly as their shared egg." Both sisters continue with their lives but with an indelible sense of absence. Desiree's shock is exacerbated by the realisation that, in some ways, she did not know Stella at all.

Divided twins are a popular trope in literature. They provide the ideal opportunity for writers to explore issues of identity, particularly the roles of nature vs nurture. Bennett acknowledges this literary tradition in her text when she alludes to Shakespeare's *Twelfth Night*. As a girl, Desiree auditions for the role of Viola—the twin who disguises herself as a boy in *Twelfth Night*. She is furious when she misses out on the role to the mayor's daughter.

Acting

Also connected to identity is the theme of acting in the novel. Stella is the most obvious example of a character who pretends to be someone else. Several of the other characters, however, are also shown to be adept actors.

Paradoxically, Kennedy only ever feels fully herself when she is performing a role. While she is never able to stick at anything else, her passion for acting endures. For Kennedy, much of the pleasure in taking on a role is the opportunity to lose herself in a different identity. Little does she know that her ability to become someone else is inherited from her mother.

Barry is another character who is drawn to perform as another persona. His motivations, however, differ from those of Kennedy and Stella. Barry does not seek to erase his own identity when he performs as drag queen Bianca. Instead, he expresses a part of himself which remains unfulfilled in his everyday role as a high school chemistry teacher. Performing as Bianca is an act of joyful creativity.

Ironically, when the Vignes twins are young, it is Desiree who dreams of becoming an actress. She is the sister who sometimes pretends to be her twin, while Stella is too afraid of getting caught. Congratulating herself on the fact that she is "a great liar," Desiree believes that she has a gift for acting that her sister lacks.

As a girl, Stella lacks the motivation to pretend to be someone else. Reserved and cautious, she has no interest in fooling those around her. Once the twins move to New Orleans, however, she is persuaded to act white for the sake of the twins' financial future. Working at Maison Blanche, she becomes Miss Vignes by day and returns to her life as Stella at night.

Stella's act differs from those of the other characters in the novel, as it is "a performance where there could be no audience." Her colleagues are blissfully unaware that she is a woman of colour and, while Desiree is in on the secret, she can never see Stella in her work environment. As Stella continues performing as Miss Vignes, she realises she does not want to share this part of her life with her twin. The role becomes a barrier which will eventually completely divide them.

By passing, Stella commits herself to living her life as a permanent performance. Unsurprisingly, the continual effort involved takes its toll on her. Often, she is unsure where her real self ends, and her role begins. As Desiree speculates, "maybe acting for that long ceased to be acting altogether. Maybe pretending to be white eventually made it so."

Vanishing & Loss

The Vanishing Half is full of vanishing or lost people. While the title refers to Stella's disappearance, there are many other instances of characters going missing. At the age of sixteen, the Vignes twins run away from Mallard in the middle of the night. Years later, Desiree performs a similar midnight flit when she leaves her violent husband. Reese runs away from his family in El Dorado to embark on life as a man. Meanwhile, Early Jones makes a living out of searching for lost people.

Most of the novel's characters disappear from their former lives in search of a better future. Those who are left behind, however, suffer a profound sense of loss and abandonment. When her twin daughters disappear, Adele is effectively left childless. Fourteen years later, Desiree returns to her, but Stella remains absent. Desiree's return is shown to be a bitter-sweet experience for Adele. While she is relieved to have one daughter back, she is also reminded afresh that there should be two: "She was supposed to have a pair. And now that one had returned, the loss of the other felt sharp and new."

Desiree's grief when Stella deserts her is particularly devastating due to the sisters' connection as twins. She is left not only alone but with a feeling of betrayal. Desiree experiences Stella's absence as a void, like missing one half of herself. When she describes Stella as having "passed over" (i.e. become white), the phrase also has connotations of death. Desiree's word choice reflects the fact that Stella is as good as dead to the loved ones who are denied contact with her for the rest of their lives. Desiree carries the loss around with them like a permanent wound.

While working as a bounty hunter, Early is continually astonished by the foolishness of wanted people who get caught when they return home for sentimental reasons. He concludes that "[t]he key to staying lost was to never love anything." This philosophy highlights the emotional detachment that is required for someone to cut all ties with their old life successfully. On the surface, Stella appears to have mastered this principle. As the novel progresses, however, it becomes clear that vanishing has left her with emotional scars.

Home

Throughout *The Vanishing Half*, identity is closely linked to the concept of home. The characters try out different places in their quest to find where they belong.

As a child, Stella has no desire to leave her hometown of Mallard. Nevertheless, she turns out to be one of the most well-travelled characters in the novel. As Stella moves from New Orleans to Boston, to Los Angeles, she becomes more entrenched in her role as a white woman and further distanced from her roots. While Stella ends up settled in the kind of luxurious house she always dreamed of, she is never entirely at home. She feels an imposter in the affluent white neighbourhood of Brentwood. Kennedy goes on to inherit her mother's sense of rootlessness. Experiencing a particular severe identity crisis, she roams around the world, pretending to be different people as she goes.

Desiree, the adventurous twin, fulfils her wish to leave Mallard. After Stella abandons her in New Orleans, she moves to Washington, D.C., where she creates a new family and home with Sam and Jude. When Sam becomes increasingly violent, however, Desiree retreats back to the hometown she once found stultifying. Now at a different stage of her life, Desiree welcomes the sense of belonging and stability she feels in Mallard, despite still disagreeing with the town's colourism.

For Desiree's daughter, Jude, Mallard is the worst possible place to grow up. As the only dark inhabitant of the town,

Jude is ostracised. When she goes to UCLA, Jude finds a spiritual home in the diversity of Los Angeles. She returns to Mallard only briefly for her grandmother's funeral.

Early Jones begins the novel as the most peripatetic of characters. With no family ties or geographical roots, he wanders the country as a bounty hunter. When he is hired to find Desiree, however, he unexpectedly finds a sense of home. Despite his negative experiences of colourism in Mallard, Early's love for Desiree draws him back to the small town again and again. Eventually, he settles there, taking a job in the local oil refinery. Early demonstrates that home can be just as much about the people who live there as the place itself.

Mother-Daughter relationships

In *The Vanishing Half*, the author portrays two generations of fraught mother-daughter relationships. The first is that between Adele and Desiree. The second is between Stella and her daughter Kennedy.

As a girl, Desiree believes her mother loves Stella the best. Obedient and pliable, Stella is an easy child while Desiree is rebellious. The more Adele tries to convince her wilder daughter to stay away from dark-skinned boys, the more attractive those boys seem. Desiree's track history means that she is the one Adele blames when the twins run away to New Orleans. Her mother also holds her culpable when Stella goes missing for good. The resulting rift between the two women lasts for many years.

During their years apart, Desiree does not inform Adele of her marriage to Sam (of which she knows her mother would disapprove), or the birth of her daughter. Meanwhile, Adele blames her mothering skills for the loss of the twins. She realises that the end result of parenting Desiree more strictly was that "Desiree felt hated and Stella felt ignored."

When Desiree returns to Mallard fourteen years later, the reunion between mother and daughter involves pride swallowing on both sides. On first greeting her daughter, Adele remains inscrutable, determined not to reveal her joy. At the same time, she does not conceal her disapproval at the dark shade of Jude's skin. Nevertheless, Adele shows her love for Desiree in small ways. Although guessing that Desiree's husband has turned violent, she refrains from saying 'I told you so.' Wordlessly, Adele expresses her empathy by presenting Desiree with mushed up cornbread and milk—her daughter's favourite comfort food as a girl.

Determined not to lose Desiree again, Adele persuades her to stay in Mallard. Mother and daughter live together for the next twenty years, and Desiree becomes Adele's carer when she has Alzheimer's. Nevertheless, their relationship does not undergo a sentimental transformation. Although the women's love for each other is evident, it remains mostly unspoken, and Desiree still feels her mother favours Stella. Her suspicions seem to be confirmed when, towards the end of her life, Adele calls Desiree by Stella's name. As the sister who stayed, Desiree finds her mother's mistake particularly hurtful. In the ultimate expression of love, however, she plays along with the scenario. When Adele asks her daughter where she went (believing she is talking to Stella), Desiree reassures her, "I never left."

Desiree's relationship with her own daughter, Jude, is less conflicted than the one she shared with her mother. This is largely because Jude, like Stella, is quiet, sensible, and studious, causing Desiree little cause for complaint. Like her aunt, however, Jude keeps her feelings to herself and privately resents her mother for taking her back to Mallard. Lacking her mother's resilience, Jude is traumatised by the colourist prejudice she faces in the town and Desiree never fully appreciates the disastrous impact on her daughter. Jude makes her mother proud by going on to UCLA and medical school. However, her success is accompanied by a geographical divide. When Desiree discovers that Jude had kept her encounter with Stella a secret, their relationship is never quite the same.

The dynamics of Adele and Desiree's mother-daughter relationship are echoed in a later generation with Stella and Kennedy. Like Desiree, Stella finds herself raising a daughter with which she has little in common. Stella feels that Kennedy should rightfully be her sister's daughter, as she is wild and impulsive.

Despite their differences, Stella loves Kennedy and longs for more intimacy with her. This connection remains evasive, however, as their relationship is built on lies. Kennedy also craves a closer relationship and is hurt by the fact that Stella refuses to talk about her early life. Kennedy concludes that her closed-off mother does not want to share anything of herself.

Much of the tension between Kennedy and her mother revolves around Stella's expectations. Having severed all ties with her family to become 'white,' Stella expects her daughter to appreciate the advantages that sacrifice has afforded. Kennedy, however, is "blissfully unaware of how hard her mother worked to maintain the lie that was her life." Stella perceives Kennedy as wasting her educational opportunities. At the same time, Kennedy sees a mother who is unsupportive of her decision to become an actor.

Some of the most painful scenes in the novel are those where Stella inflicts her conflicted racial values on her young daughter. When Stella tells Kennedy not to play with "niggers," she teaches her daughter to be racist. When Kennedy repeats the same racist sentiments to Cindy, however, Stella slaps her and then kisses her daughter to apologise. Readers know that Stella's actions are prompted by fear of exposure. For Kennedy, however, both scenarios are equally confusing. She is left with the sense that she has misbehaved when Stella is the one at fault. Poignantly, Kennedy is more surprised when her mother kisses her than by the slap that precedes it.

The novel's treatment of mothers and their daughters highlights the fact that these relationships are rarely straightforward. Both sides crave an easy intimacy, but conflicting personalities and parental expectations make this difficult to achieve. While the mothers and daughters clash in *The Vanishing Half*, Bennett makes it clear that these conflicts never arise from a lack of love.

The River

The Vanishing Half ends with Jude and Reese taking their clothes off and wading in the river. In this scene, the river takes on baptismal symbolism, implying a fresh start for both characters. By unselfconsciously stripping naked, Jude and Reese demonstrate that they have overcome the feelings of self-loathing their bodies once inspired in them. Doing so in Mallard—the site of Jude's traumatic upbringing—suggests that they are washing away the oppression of their past. By concluding the novel with this image, Bennett hints that the younger generation have the power to move beyond their inherited history.

Colour

Throughout the novel, colour symbolism is playfully used to underline the themes of racism and colourism. When Stella first commits to passing, for example, it is to work at Maison Blanche. Translated from French, Maison Blanche means 'White House'— an appropriate name for a department store which does not admit black staff or customers. White is also the surname of the president of the residents' association who tries to boycott a black family from moving into the neighbourhood. Even Stella's married name, Sanders, has subtle racial connotations. It reflects the fact that her ambiguous sandy "beige" skin tone allows her to pass as a white woman.

Broken Glass

Bennett uses the image of broken glass at several dramatic

points in her storyline. At a Beverly Hills party, Jude drops a bottle of red wine when she first sees Stella. Guests stare as Jude picks up the shards of glass, and she is fired for the offence. In another scene, Stella breaks a wine glass after Loretta's black friends astutely imply that she is a poor friend to her neighbour. This moment is later echoed after Stella makes unfounded allegations about Reginald. As a result, bricks are thrown through the Walkers' window, shattering the glass and injuring Cindy. It is no accident that all of these incidents are linked to Stella. The broken glass imagery hints at the harm she inadvertently causes through her life of deceit.

DISCUSSION QUESTIONS

1/ The narrative perspective of *The Vanishing Half* shifts between different characters. Which character did you like best and whose viewpoint did you find most interesting? Were some characters more fully realised than others?

2/ The story primarily focuses on two generations of women: Stella and Desiree, and their daughters, Kennedy and Jude. Which generation did you find yourself most invested in, and why?

3/ The novel covers four decades and skips back and forth in time, sometimes within the space of a single chapter. Why does the author use this technique? Is it effective?

4/ Discuss the way growing up as a twin affects Stella and Desiree's sense of who they are. Which sister is more dependent on the other?

5/ Leon Vignes is murdered by white men when his twin daughters are still very young. How does this traumatic event go on to shape Stella and Desiree?

6/ The small town of Mallard is described as "more idea than place." What does the author mean by this? How does growing up in Mallard affect the Vignes twins and, later, Desiree's daughter, Jude? What do the people of Mallard gain from their colourist attitude to skin tone?

7/ As a child, Desiree loves acting and sometimes pretends to be Stella. Given her love of performing, why does Desiree never consider passing as white?

8/ As young women, the Vignes twins take contrasting paths in life. How do their respective fates underline the racial injustices of American society?

9/ Discuss the impact Stella's decision to pass as white has on Adele and Desiree. Why does Stella feel the need to cut all contact with her family? Would you have done the same in her shoes?

10/ Stella gains social and economic advantages by pretending to be white. What impact does it have on her relationships and sense of self?

11/ In her adult life, Stella is shown to be closed-off and deceitful. Do readers get to see a glimmer of another personality beneath the veneer of "White Stella?"

12/ By successfully pretending to be a white woman, Stella fools the white people around her. Can Stella's decision to pass be seen as a defiance of white supremacy, or does she simply reinforce the racial status quo?

13/ Discuss Blake Sanders' attitude to race and racism. How do you think he would have reacted if he had discovered his wife's secret?

14/ After leaving her husband, Desiree returns to Mallard, despite knowing how the residents are likely to react to Jude. Why do you think she makes this decision? Is it a mistake?

15/ Jude and Kennedy are raised in completely contrasting environments. How does their upbringing shape the people they become? Why do you think, at the end of the novel, the cousins choose to remain secretly in touch with each other?

16/ When a black family buys a property in her neighbourhood, Stella draws attention to herself by protesting at a residents' association meeting. Why does she react so dramatically to the arrival of the Walkers? How did you feel about her use of the n-word when ordering Kennedy not to play with Cindy Walker?

17/ Despite opposing the Walkers' arrival in Brentwood, Stella finds herself drawn to Loretta Walker. Why does Stella find her neighbour so compelling? Do you think Stella would ever have given in to the temptation to tell Loretta her secret?

18/ How does Reginald Walker's TV persona affect the way he is initially treated in Brentwood? Why do the residents react so violently when Stella claims she does not like the way Reginald looks at her? Do you think Stella anticipates this reaction?

19/ Several of the characters are drawn to acting or transforming themselves in one way or another. How does Stella's performance as a white woman differ from Reese's role as a transgender man, Barry's drag act, or Kennedy's acting roles? What is the author suggesting about identity?

20/ How does Stella and Blake's marriage compare with the relationships between Desiree and Early, and Reese and Jude? What part does authenticity play in each partnership?

21/ How did you feel about Stella's brief return to Mallard? Would it have been better for everyone concerned if she had never returned at all?

22/ Much of the tension of the novel's plot revolves around whether Stella will be found out. In the end, although Kennedy discovers her secret, Stella is never publicly exposed as an imposter. Why do you think the author makes this choice?

23/ Which of the Vignes twins do you believe ends up leading a fuller life?

24/ Why does the author end the novel with the image of Jude and Reese wading in the river? How did you feel about this ending?

25/ The passing genre was popular in the early twentieth century. Why does Brit Bennett choose to adopt it? Are the genre's themes of race and colourism still just as relevant today?

26/ How many stars would you give *The Vanishing Half*? Will you recommend it to friends?

QUIZ QUESTIONS

1/ As the novel opens, which famous figure has recently been assassinated?

2/ What is the name of the diner in Mallard?

3/ Which of Shakespeare's plays does Desiree audition for as a girl?

4/ How old are the twins when they run away to New Orleans?

5/ What is the name of the department store where Stella works as a secretary?

6/ How does Stella meet Blake?

7/ What colour are Kennedy's eyes?

8/ Early fails in only two of his missions to find lost people. Which ones?

9/ What is the name of the speakeasy in Mallard?

10/ What is Reese's birthname?

11/ Name Barry's alter ego.

12/ Why does Stella disapprove of Kennedy's boyfriend, Frantz?

13/ What does Reginald Walker do for a living?

14/ Why does Percy White throw a brick through the Walkers' window?

15/ When Stella briefly returns to Mallard, what does she ask Early to sell?

QUIZ ANSWERS

1/ Martin Luther King Jr.

2/ Lou's Egg House

3/ *Twelfth Night*

4/ Sixteen

5/ Maison Blanche

6/ He is her boss

7/ Violet

8/ He does not find Stella. He also fails to trace his parents as he does not know enough about them.

9/ The Surly Goat

10/ Therese Anne Carter

11/ Bianca, the drag queen

12/ He is black

13/ He is an actor, famous for playing a police officer on a popular TV drama

14/ Stella claims Reginald looks at her in a way that makes her feel "uncomfortable."

15/ Her diamond wedding ring

FURTHER READING

Fiction

The Mothers by Brit Bennett

Passing by Nella Larsen

The Bluest Eye by Toni Morrison

Tar Baby by Toni Morrison

God Help the Child by Toni Morrison

Their Eyes Were Watching God by Zora Neale Hurston

Mrs. Everything by Jennifer Weiner

Such a Fun Age by Kiley Reid

Nonfiction

Caste by Isabel Wilkerson

We Wear the Mask: 15 True Stories of Passing in America edited by Brando Skyhorse & Lisa Page

FURTHER GUIDES IN THIS SERIES

Alias Grace (Margaret Atwood)

American Dirt (Jeanine Cummins)

Beartown (Fredrik Backman)

Before We Were Yours (Lisa Wingate)

Big Little Lies (Liane Moriarty)

The Book Thief (Markus Zusak)

Circe (Madeline Miller)

Commonwealth (Ann Patchett)

Educated (Tara Westover)

The Fault in Our Stars (John Green)

Frankenstein (Mary Shelley)

A Gentleman in Moscow (Amor Towles)

The Girl on the Train (Paula Hawkins)

Go Set a Watchman (Harper Lee)

A God in Ruins (Kate Atkinson)

The Goldfinch (Donna Tartt)

Gone Girl (Gillian Flynn)

The Great Alone (Kristin Hannah)

The Great Gatsby (F. Scott Fitzgerald)

The Grownup (Gillian Flynn)

The Guernsey Literary and Potato Peel Pie Society (Mary Ann Shaffer & Annie Burrows)

The Handmaid's Tale (Margaret Atwood

The Heart Goes Last (Margaret Atwood)

The Husband's Secret (Liane Moriarty)

I Know Why the Caged Bird Sings (Maya Angelou)

The Light between Oceans (M.L. Stedman)

Lincoln in the Bardo (George Saunders)

Little Fires Everywhere (Celeste Ng)

My Brilliant Friend (Elena Ferrante)

My Name is Lucy Barton (Elizabeth Strout)

The Narrow Road to the Deep North (Richard Flanagan)

The Nickel Boys (Colson Whitehead)

Normal People (Sally Rooney)

Olive, Again (Elizabeth Strout)

The Overstory (Richard Powers)

Pachinko (Min Jin Lee)

The Paying Guests (Sarah Waters)

The Secret History (Donna Tartt)

The Storied Life of A.J. Fikry (Gabrielle Zevin)

The Sympathizer (Viet Thanh Nguyen)

The Testaments (Margaret Atwood)

The Underground Railroad (Colson Whitehead)

Where the Crawdads Sing (Delia Owens)

BIBLIOGRAPHY

Books

Bennett, Brit. *The Vanishing Half.* Riverhead Books, 2020

Articles

ABC News (1 November 2005). "Skin-deep discrimination." *Abcnews.go.com.* Retrieved October 10, 2020

Bennett, Brit (December 17 2014). "I Don't Know What to Do With Good White People." *Jezebel.* Retrieved October 15 2020.

Biggs, Joanna (13 August 2020). "What she wasn't." *London Review of Books.* Retrieved October 15, 2020.

Bradbury, Janine (20 August 2018). "Passing for white: how a taboo film genre is being revived to expose racial privilege." *The Guardian.* Retrieved October 15, 2020.

Canfield, David (3 June 2020). "The Vanishing Half explores race and identity in America. It's timeless— and urgent: Review." *Entertainment Weekly.* Retrieved October 10, 2020.

Crawford, Maria (17 June 2020). "The Vanishing Half — painful truths about race and skin colour in America." *Financial Times.* Retrieved October 15, 2020.

Donkor, Michael (4 June 2020). "The Vanishing Half Brit Bennett review — a twin's struggle to pass for white." *The Guardian.* Retrieved October 15, 2020

Grady, Constance (14 Aug 2020). "How The Vanishing Half fits into our cultural fixation with racial passing stories." *Vox*. Retrieved October 10, 2020.

Grant, Colin (23 June 2020). "The Vanishing Half Brit Bennet review — two faces of the black experience." *The Guardian*. Retrieved October 15, 2020.

Mathis, Ayana (29 May 2020). "A Novel Imagines the Fate of Twin Sisters, One Passing for White." *The New York Times*. Retrieved October 13, 2020.

McAlpin, Heller (3 June 2020). "The Vanishing Half Counts The Terrible Costs Of Bigotry And Secrecy." *NPR*. Retrieved October 12, 2020.

Page, Lisa (1 June 2020). "Brit Bennett's 'The Vanishing Half' is a fierce examination of passing and the price people pay for a new identity." *The Washington Post*. Retrieved October 12, 2020.

Patrick, Bethanne (28 May 2020). "Review: 'The Vanishing Half' reveals novelist Brit Bennett in full." *Los Angeles Times*. Retrieved October 12, 2020.

Resnick, Sarah (15 June 2020). "Brit Bennett Reimagines the Literature of Passing." *The New Yorker*. Retrieved October 10, 2020.

Sehgal, Parul (26 May 2020). "Brit Bennett's New Novel Explores the Power and Performance of Race." *The New York Times*. Retrieved October 10, 2020.

Shapiro, Lila (12 June 2020). "If You Can Perform Whiteness, Then What Does It Mean to Be White?" *Vulture*. Retrieved October 13, 2020.

Vanderhoof, Erin (5 June 2020). "Now That Someone Has Given You This Knowledge, What Are You Going to Do With It?: Brit Bennett on The Vanishing Half, Protest, and How Change Happens." *Vanity Fair*. Retrieved October 12, 2020.

Websites

https://britbennett.com/

ABOUT THE AUTHOR

Kathryn Cope has a degree in English Literature from Manchester University and a master's degree in contemporary fiction from the University of York. She is the author of Study Guides for Book Clubs and the HarperCollins Official Book Club guides. She lives in the Staffordshire Moorlands with her husband, son and dog.

Lightning Source UK Ltd.
Milton Keynes UK
UKHW010130061021
391693UK00002B/409